HAL•LEONARD

JAZZ PLAY-ALONG®

Book and CD for B♭, E♭, C and Bass Clef Instruments

volume
101

Arranged and Produced by
Mark Taylor

Bud Powell

10 Classic Tunes

Photo by William "PoPsie" Randolph
www.PoPsiePhotos.com

ISBN 978-1-4234-6388-7

HAL•LEONARD®
CORPORATION

7777 W. BLUEMOUND RD. P.O. BOX 13819 MILWAUKEE, WI 53213

Visit Hal Leonard Online at
www.halleonard.com

BUD POWELL

Volume 101

Arranged and Produced
by Mark Taylor

Featured Players:

Graham Breedlove–Trumpet
John Desalme–Saxes
Tony Nalker–Piano
Jim Roberts–Bass
Joe McCarthy–Drums

Recorded at Bias Studios, Springfield, Virginia
Bob Dawson, Engineer

HOW TO USE THE CD:

Each song has <u>two</u> tracks:

1) Split Track/Melody

Woodwind, Brass, Keyboard, and **Mallet Players** can use this track as a learning tool for melody style and inflection.

Bass Players can learn and perform with this track – remove the recorded bass track by turning down the volume on the LEFT channel.

Keyboard and **Guitar Players** can learn and perform with this track – remove the recorded piano part by turning down the volume on the RIGHT channel.

2) Full Stereo Track

Soloists or **Groups** can learn and perform with this accompaniment track with the RHYTHM SECTION only.

CD
1 : SPLIT TRACK/MELODY
2 : FULL STEREO TRACK

BOUNCING WITH BUD

WORDS AND MUSIC BY EARL "BUD" POWELL
AND WALTER GIL FULLER

C VERSION

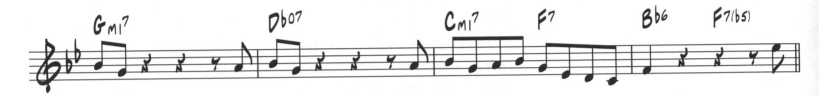

BUSTER RIDES AGAIN

BY EARL "BUD" POWELL

CD
- ③ : SPLIT TRACK/MELODY
- ④ : FULL STEREO TRACK

C VERSION

DANCE OF THE INFIDELS

CD
◆5: SPLIT TRACK/MELODY
◆6: FULL STEREO TRACK

BY EARL "BUD" POWELL

C VERSION

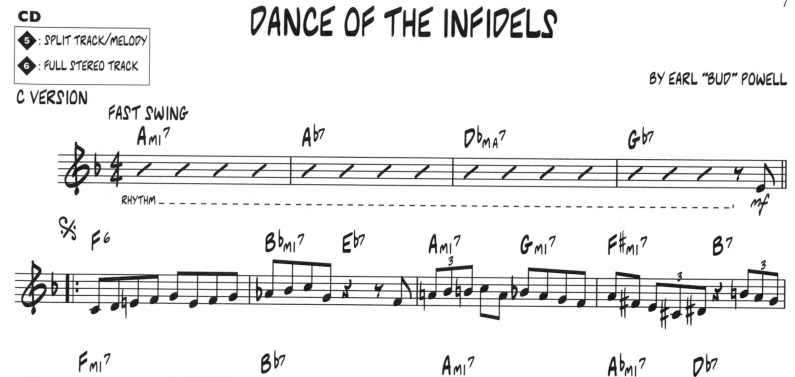

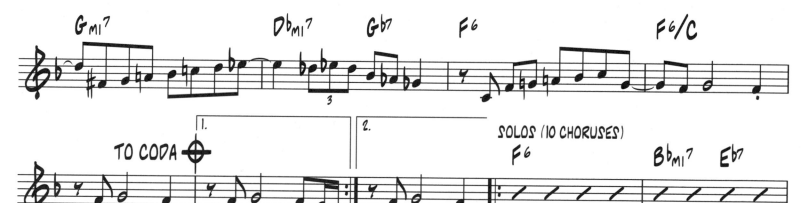

ELOGIE

BY EARL "BUD" POWELL

CD
7: SPLIT TRACK/MELODY
8: FULL STEREO TRACK

C VERSION

9

SOLOS (3 CHORUSES)

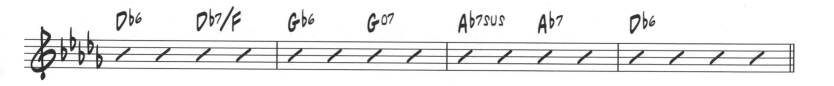

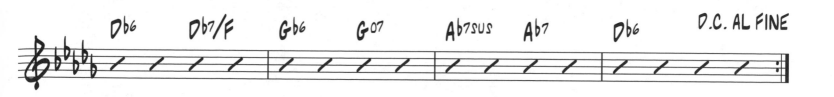

HALLUCINATIONS

BY EARL "BUD" POWELL

C VERSION

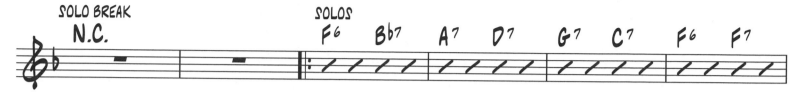

SOLO BREAK
N.C.   SOLOS

D.C. AL CODA
TAKE REPEAT

CODA

PARISIAN THOROUGHFARE

BY EARL "BUD" POWELL

CD
13 : SPLIT TRACK/MELODY
14 : FULL STEREO TRACK

C VERSION

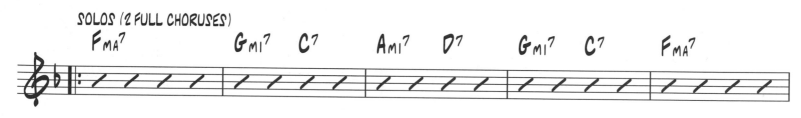

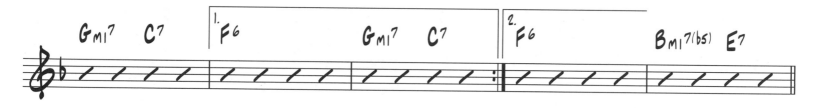

SO SORRY PLEASE

CD
15 : SPLIT TRACK/MELODY
16 : FULL STEREO TRACK

C VERSION

BY EARL "BUD" POWELL

MEDIUM SWING

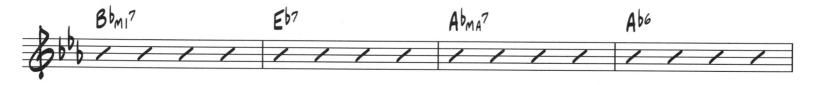

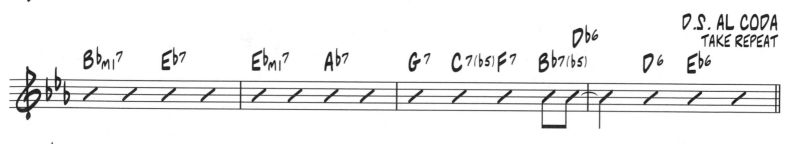

UN POCO LOCO

BY EARL "BUD" POWELL

C VERSION

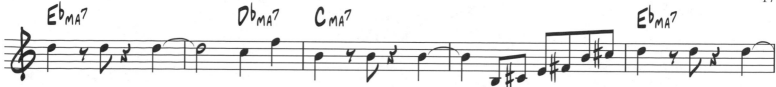

WAIL

BY EARL "BUD" POWELL

C VERSION

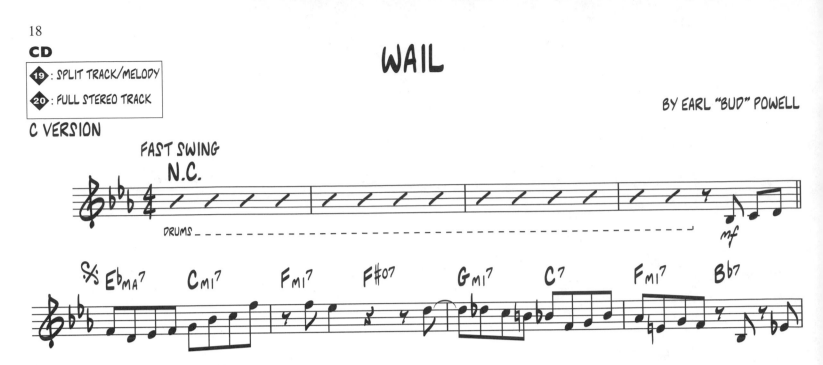

TO CODA
Ebma7 Eb7/Db Cmi7 Abmi7/Cb Bb7 Bb+7 Eb6 Bb+7
SOLO (3 CHORUSES)
Ebma7 Cmi7 Fmi7 F#o7 Gmi7 C7 Fmi7 Bb7
Ebma7 Eb7/G Ab6 Ao7 Ebma7/Bb C7 Fmi7 Bb7(b5)
Ebma7 Cmi7 Fmi7 F#o7 Gmi7 C7 F7 Bb7 Ebma7 Eb7/Db
Cmi7 Abmi7/Cb Bb7 Eb6 Gmi7(b5)
C7(b5) Fmi7(b5) Bb7(b5)
Ebma7 Cmi7 Fmi7 F#o7 Gmi7 C7 F7 Bb7
D.S. AL CODA
LAST TIME
Ebma7 Eb7/Db Cmi7 Abmi7/Cb Bb7 Eb6 Bb+7
LAST X ONLY
CODA Eb6 Db6 D7 Eb6

OBLIVION

BY EARL "BUD" POWELL

OBLIVION

BY EARL "BUD" POWELL

Bb VERSION

BOUNCING WITH BUD

WORDS AND MUSIC BY EARL "BUD" POWELL
AND WALTER GIL FULLER

CD

① : SPLIT TRACK/MELODY
② : FULL STEREO TRACK

Bb VERSION

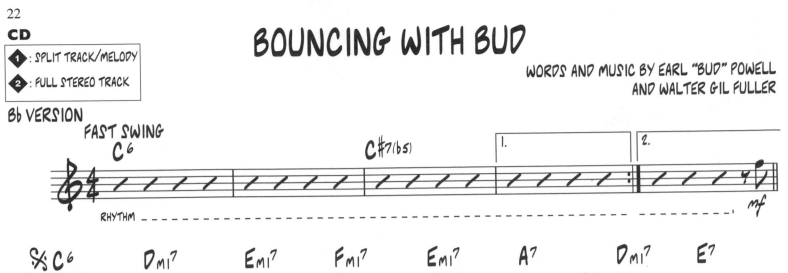

BUSTER RIDES AGAIN

BY EARL "BUD" POWELL

Bb VERSION

DANCE OF THE INFIDELS

BY EARL "BUD" POWELL

CD
◆5: SPLIT TRACK/MELODY
◆6: FULL STEREO TRACK

Bb VERSION

CD

7 : SPLIT TRACK/MELODY
8 : FULL STEREO TRACK

ELOGIE

BY EARL "BUD" POWELL

Bb VERSION

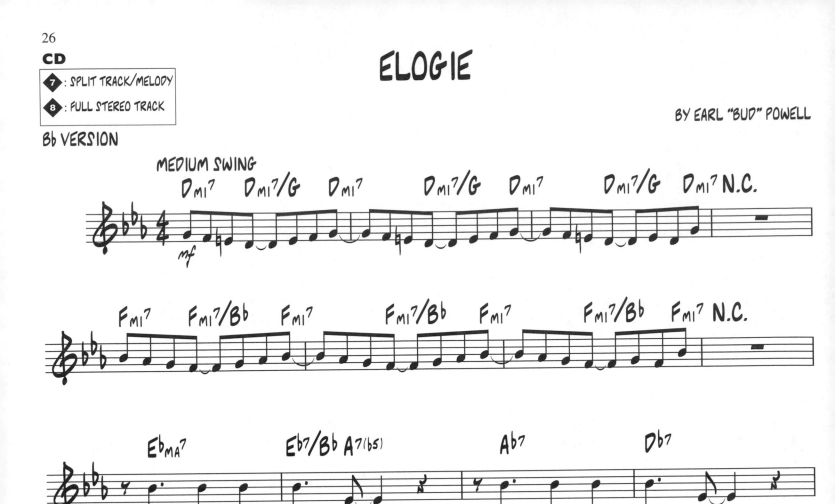

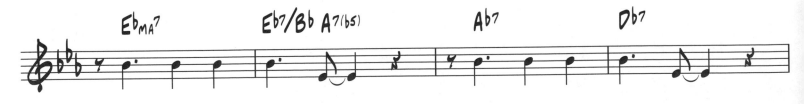

SOLOS (3 CHORUSES)

HALLUCINATIONS

CD
9: SPLIT TRACK/MELODY
10: FULL STEREO TRACK

BY EARL "BUD" POWELL

Bb VERSION

TO CODA ⊕

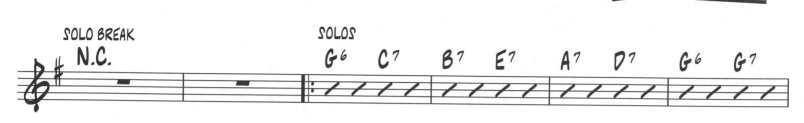

SOLO BREAK
N.C.

SOLOS
G⁶ C⁷ B⁷ E⁷ A⁷ D⁷ G⁶ G⁷

C⁶ C#°7 G⁷/D E⁷ Am1⁷ D⁷ G⁶ D⁷ G⁶ C⁷ B⁷ E⁷

A⁷ D⁷ G⁶ G⁷ C⁶ C#°7 G⁷/D E⁷ Am1⁷ D⁷ G⁶ F⁷

Em1⁷ A⁷ Dm1⁷ G⁷ Cm1⁷ F⁷ Bm1⁷ E⁷ Am1 E⁷/B C⁶ D⁷

G⁶ E⁷ Am1⁷ D⁷ C#m1⁷(b5)C⁷ B⁷ E⁷ A⁷ D⁷

D.C. AL CODA
TAKE REPEAT

G⁶ G⁷ C⁶ C#°7 G⁷/D E⁷ Am1⁷ D⁷ G⁶ D⁷

⊕ CODA G⁶ G⁷ C⁷ C#°7 G⁷/D

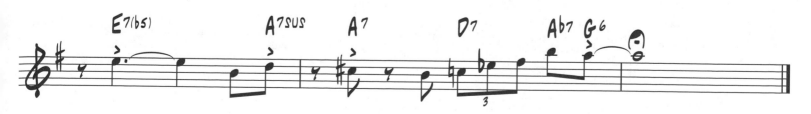

PARISIAN THOROUGHFARE

BY EARL "BUD" POWELL

CD
13: SPLIT TRACK/MELODY
14: FULL STEREO TRACK

Bb VERSION

CD
15 : SPLIT TRACK/MELODY
16 : FULL STEREO TRACK

SO SORRY PLEASE

BY EARL "BUD" POWELL

Bb VERSION

UN POCO LOCO

BY EARL "BUD" POWELL

CD
- **17** : SPLIT TRACK/MELODY
- **18** : FULL STEREO TRACK

Bb VERSION

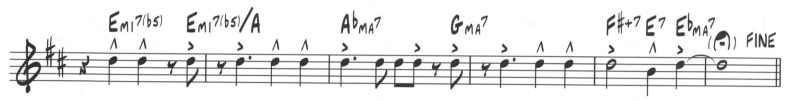

CD
19 : SPLIT TRACK/MELODY
20 : FULL STEREO TRACK

WAIL

BY EARL "BUD" POWELL

Bb VERSION

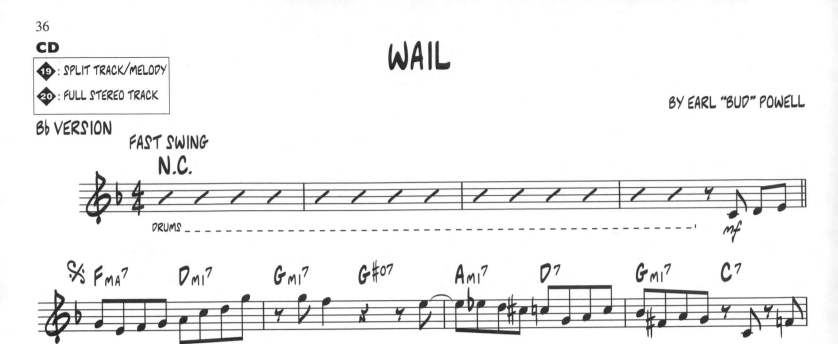

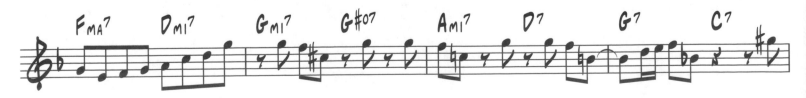

TO CODA ⊕

F MA7   F7/Eb   D mi7   Bbmi7/Db   C7   C +7/3   F6   C +7

SOLO (3 CHORUSES)
F MA7   D mi7   G mi7   G#07   A mi7   D7   G mi7   C7

F MA7   F7/A   Bb6   B07   F MA7/C   D7   G mi7   C7(b5)

F MA7   D mi7   G mi7   G#07   A mi7   D7   G7   C7   F MA7   F7/Eb

D mi7   Bbmi7/Db C7   F6   A mi7(b5)

D7(b5)   G mi7(b5)   C7(b5)

F MA7   D mi7   G mi7   G#07   A mi7   D7   G7   C7

D.S. AL CODA
LAST TIME

F MA7   F7/Eb   D mi7   Bbmi7/Db   C7   F6   C +7

LAST X ONLY

⊕ CODA F6   Eb6   E7   F6

CD

1 : SPLIT TRACK/MELODY
2 : FULL STEREO TRACK

BOUNCING WITH BUD

WORDS AND MUSIC BY EARL "BUD" POWELL
AND WALTER GIL FULLER

Eb VERSION

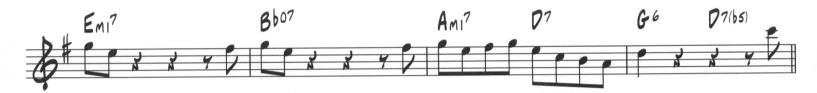

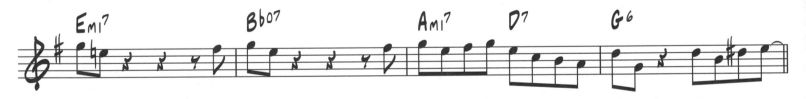

BUSTER RIDES AGAIN

BY EARL "BUD" POWELL

Eb VERSION

Dance of the Infidels

CD
5 : SPLIT TRACK/MELODY
6 : FULL STEREO TRACK

BY EARL "BUD" POWELL

Eb VERSION

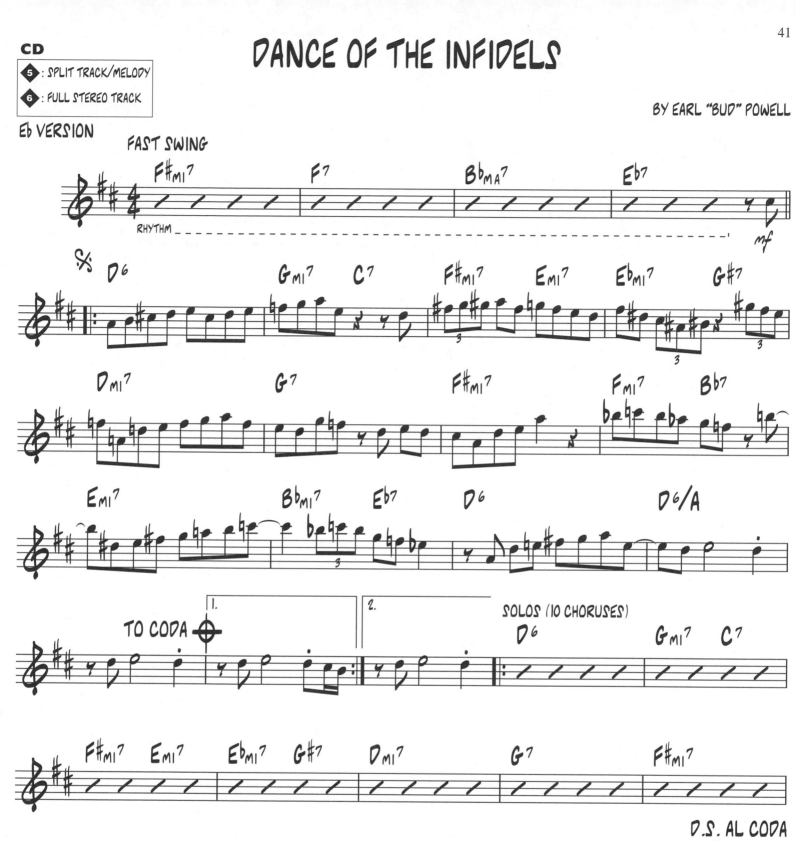

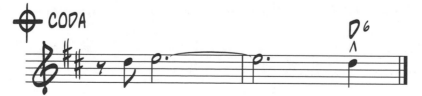

ELOGIE

CD
- **7**: SPLIT TRACK/MELODY
- **8**: FULL STEREO TRACK

BY EARL "BUD" POWELL

Eb VERSION

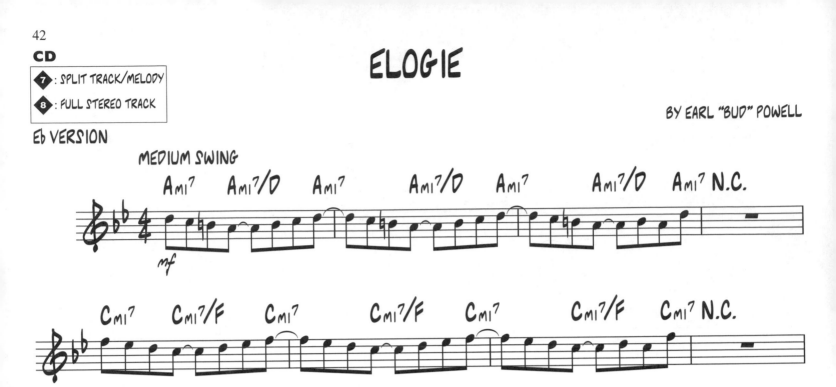

SOLOS (3 CHORUSES)

HALLUCINATIONS

CD
◆9: SPLIT TRACK/MELODY
◆10: FULL STEREO TRACK

BY EARL "BUD" POWELL

Eb VERSION

TO CODA ⊕

SOLO BREAK
N.C.

SOLOS
D6 G7 F#7 B7 E7 A7 D6 D7

G6 G#o7 D7/A B7 Em7 A7 D6 A7 D6 G7 F#7 B7

E7 A7 D6 D7 G6 G#o7 D7/A B7 Em7 A7 D6 C7

Bm7 E7 Am7 D7 Gm7 C7 F#m7 B7 Em1 B7/F# G6 A7

D6 B7 Em7 A7 G#m7(b5) G7 F#7 B7 E7 A7

D.C. AL CODA
TAKE REPEAT

D6 D7 G6 G#o7 D7/A B7 Em7 A7 D6 A7

⊕ CODA D6   D7   G7   G#o7   D7/A

PARISIAN THOROUGHFARE

CD
13 : SPLIT TRACK/MELODY
14 : FULL STEREO TRACK

BY EARL "BUD" POWELL

Eb VERSION

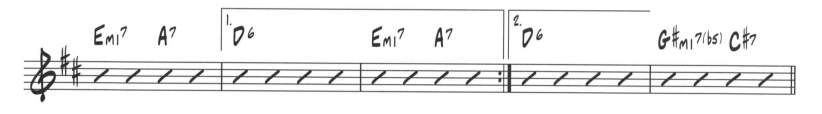

SO SORRY PLEASE

BY EARL "BUD" POWELL

Eb VERSION

TO CODA
Gmi7 C7 Cmi7 F7 E7 A7(b5) D7 Bb6 G7(b5) B6 C6
SOLO
C6 Ami7 Dmi7 G+7 Emi7 A7 Dmi7 G+7 Gmi7 C7
Cmi7 F7 1. Emi7 Eb7 Dmi7 G+7 2. Dmi7 G+7 C6
Gmi7 C7 Fma7 F6
Ami7 D7 Gmi7 Eb7 Dmi7 C#7
C6 Ami7 Dmi7 G+7 Emi7 A7 Dmi7 G+7
Gmi7 C7 Cmi7 F7 E7 A7(b5) D7 Bb6 G7(b5) B6 C6
D.S. AL CODA
TAKE REPEAT
CODA
B6 C6 Bb6 B6 C6 Bb6 B6 C6 Bb6 B6 C6

CD

17 : SPLIT TRACK/MELODY
18 : FULL STEREO TRACK

UN POCO LOCO

BY EARL "BUD" POWELL

E♭ VERSION

WAIL

BY EARL "BUD" POWELL

CD
19 : SPLIT TRACK/MELODY
20 : FULL STEREO TRACK

Eb VERSION

TO CODA
CMA7 C7/Bb AMI7 FMI7/Ab G7 G+7 C6 G+7
SOLO (3 CHORUSES)
CMA7 AMI7 DMI7 D#07 EMI7 A7 DMI7 G7
CMA7 C7/E F6 F#07 CMA7/G A7 DMI7 G7(b5)
CMA7 AMI7 DMI7 D#07 EMI7 A7 D7 G7 CMA7 C7/Bb
AMI7 FMI7/Ab G7 C6 EMI7(b5)
A7(b5) DMI7(b5) G7(b5)
CMA7 AMI7 DMI7 D#07 EMI7 A7 D7 G7
D.S. AL CODA
LAST TIME
CMA7 C7/Bb AMI7 FMI7/Ab G7 C6 G+7
LAST X ONLY
CODA
C6 Bb6 B7 C6

OBLIVION

BY EARL "BUD" POWELL

OBLIVION

BY EARL "BUD" POWELL

BOUNCING WITH BUD

WORDS AND MUSIC BY EARL "BUD" POWELL
AND WALTER GIL FULLER

CD
🔊 : SPLIT TRACK/MELODY
🔊 : FULL STEREO TRACK

🎼: C VERSION

BUSTER RIDES AGAIN

BY EARL "BUD" POWELL

DANCE OF THE INFIDELS

BY EARL "BUD" POWELL

ELOGIE

BY EARL "BUD" POWELL

𝄢: C VERSION

SOLOS (3 CHORUSES)

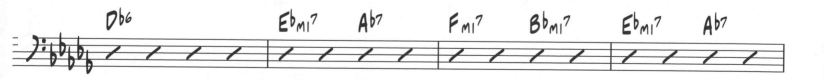

HALLUCINATIONS

BY EARL "BUD" POWELL

PARISIAN THOROUGHFARE

BY EARL "BUD" POWELL

SOLOS (2 FULL CHORUSES)

D.S. AL CODA
TAKE REPEAT

LAST X ONLY

CODA

CD

SO SORRY PLEASE

BY EARL "BUD" POWELL

𝄢: C VERSION

MEDIUM SWING

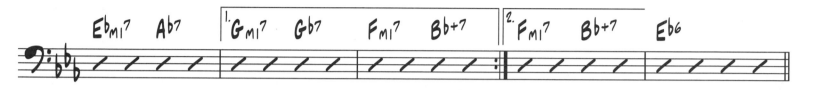

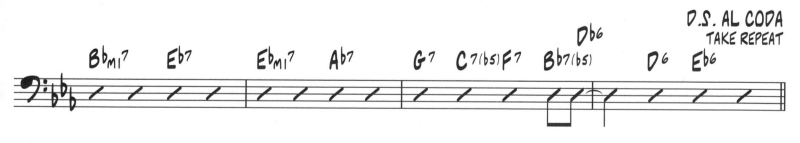

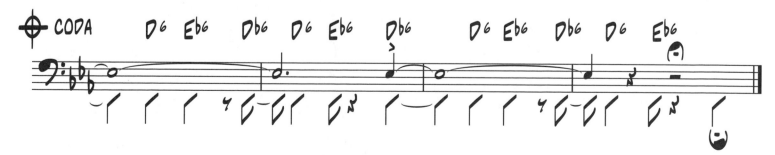

UN POCO LOCO

BY EARL "BUD" POWELL

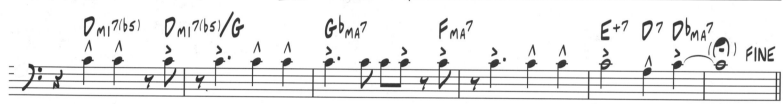

CD

19 : SPLIT TRACK/MELODY
20 : FULL STEREO TRACK

WAIL

BY EARL "BUD" POWELL

𝄢: C VERSION

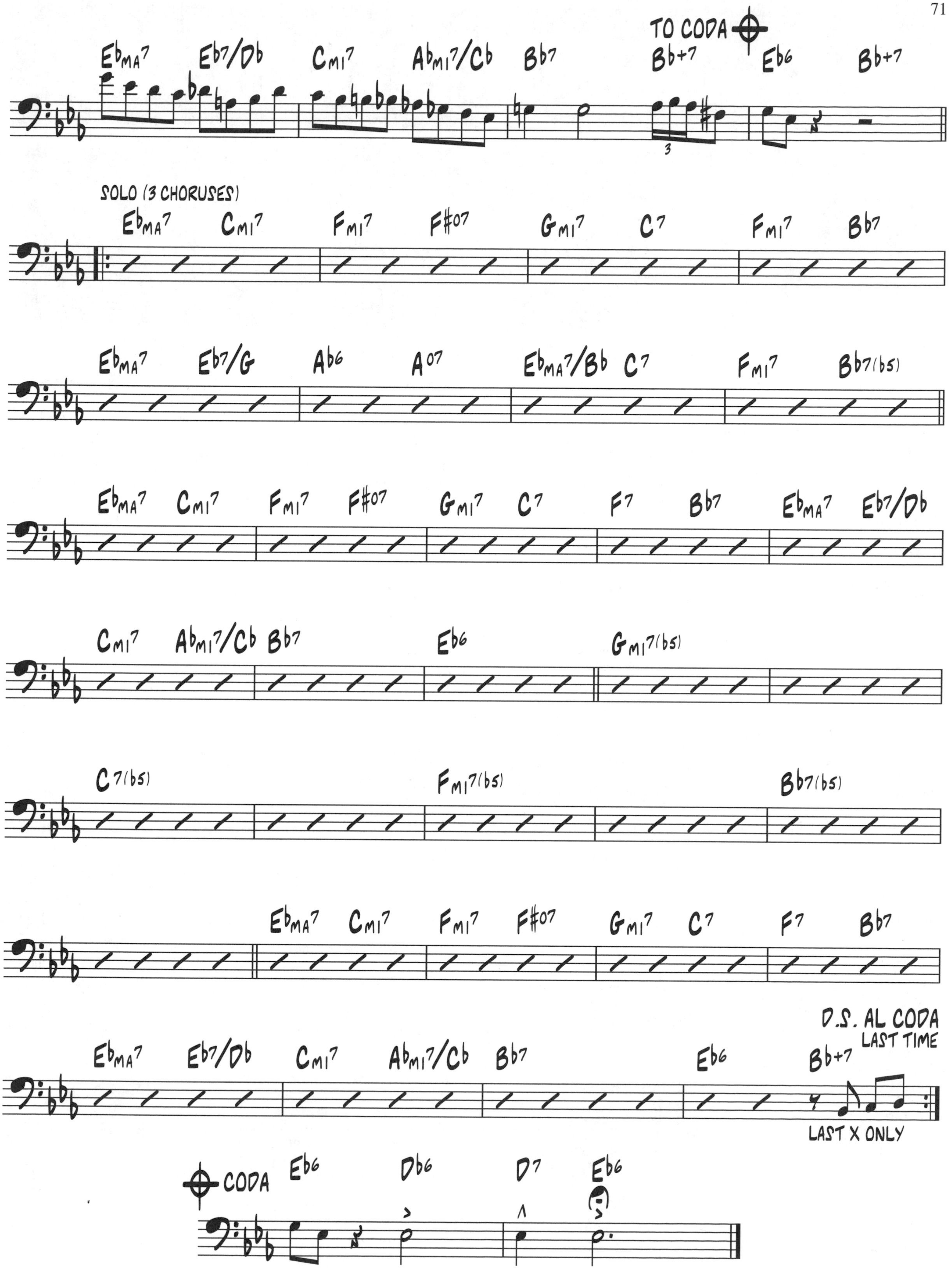
TO CODA
Ebma7 Eb7/Db Cmi7 Abmi7/Cb Bb7 Bb+7 Eb6 Bb+7
3
SOLO (3 CHORUSES)
Ebma7 Cmi7 Fmi7 F#o7 Gmi7 C7 Fmi7 Bb7
Ebma7 Eb7/G Ab6 Ao7 Ebma7/Bb C7 Fmi7 Bb7(b5)
Ebma7 Cmi7 Fmi7 F#o7 Gmi7 C7 F7 Bb7 Ebma7 Eb7/Db
Cmi7 Abmi7/Cb Bb7 Eb6 Gmi7(b5)
C7(b5) Fmi7(b5) Bb7(b5)
Ebma7 Cmi7 Fmi7 F#o7 Gmi7 C7 F7 Bb7
D.S. AL CODA
LAST TIME
Ebma7 Eb7/Db Cmi7 Abmi7/Cb Bb7 Eb6 Bb+7
LAST X ONLY
CODA
Eb6 Db6 D7 Eb6